MW00959162

FOUNDATIONS SERIES / BOOK 1 | FOUN...

The

GOSPEL

JONATHAN K. DODSON

Series editors: Rob Berreth & Claude Atcho

THE
GOSPEL

JONATHAN K. DODSON
Series editors: Rob Berreth & Claude Atcho

Foundations: The Gospel

Copyright © 2023 by Jonathan Dodson

Cover design and typesetting by Brittany Schrock

First printing 2023

All emphases in Scripture quotations have been added by the author.

CONTENTS

FOUNDATIONS
SERIES

Welcome to Foundations, a comprehensive series designed to explore the foundational elements of the Christian faith. Whether you are a new Christian seeking to deepen your understanding of your faith, a seasoned Christian eager to revisit or learn how to pass on the bedrock principles of your faith, or you are just exploring what the Christian faith is, this series is crafted with you in mind.

The Journey Ahead

Our series is divided into four distinct areas, each encompassing three books.

Christian Story	Christian Belief	Christian Practice	Christian Mission
1. The Gospel	2. The Bible	3. Devotion	4. Mission
5. Worldview	6. Doctrine	7. The Church	8. Relationships
9. Humanity	10. Ethics	11. Maturity	12. Discipleship

These areas are not merely academic divisions but practical guides to living out your faith in the real world.

LET'S TAKE A CLOSER LOOK

1. Christian Story

In Christian Story, we delve into the heart of Christianity. We explore the gospel, the Christian worldview, and the nature of humanity. These foundational concepts provide the context for your faith and all of existence.

2. Christian Belief

Here we dive into the Bible, Christian doctrine, and ethics. These books will give you a solid understanding of the core teachings that underpin your faith.

3. Christian Practice

Christian Practice covers devotion, the role of the church, and the journey towards spiritual maturity. You will discover practical ways to cultivate your faith and grow in your walk with Christ.

4. Christian Mission

Christian Mission encompasses evangelism, building meaningful relationships, and the art of discipleship. These topics empower you to actively engage with the world around you and live out your faith with others.

A JOURNEY
OF COMMUNITY

While these books can be read independently, we encourage you to embark on this journey with others. Faith is a communal experience, and we believe that reading and discussing these topics with others will have a greater impact than doing so alone.

YOUR PATH TO
REAL-WORLD DISCIPLESHIP

Foundations is not just a series of books. It is a roadmap for real-world discipleship. Together, we will explore the rich tapestry of Christian beliefs, practices, and mission. As you embark on this journey through the foundational elements of our faith, we pray that your heart may be stirred for Christ, your mind enlightened by Christ, your faith deepened in Christ, and all by the grace of Christ.

HOW TO GET THE MOST OUT OF THIS BOOK

To help maximize your experience and transformation, we encourage you to follow the rhythm below for each chapter of the book.

1. Read one chapter.
While you can read at any pace, we recommend one chapter per week. Consider praying before you start reading, asking the Holy Spirit to give insight as you work through the material

2. Reflect on what you read.
Each chapter will feature a set of questions designed to help you process the content to increase learning, application, and ownership of the material.

3. Reflect on key bible passages.

Knowing what the Bible says about the topic of each chapter is paramount. Each chapter will include key biblical passages for further reading and reflection.

4. Discuss the reflection questions with others.

While the books that comprise the Foundations series can be read independently, we encourage you to engage them with others. When you gather, pray together, read the key bible passages, and discuss the reflection questions.

5. Complete the key project.

Each Foundations book will include a key project, or two, to help you synthesize what you have learned. We encourage you to complete it by the time you finish the book, and then discuss it at your final group gathering.

There is one project for this book.

Written Personal Definition of the Gospel and Personal Testimony in Light of It

Write a definition of the gospel that is in your own words, but that also takes your learnings from the book into account. Additionally, write your personal testimony in such a way that it becomes a real-life demonstration of your personal definition of the gospel.

CHAPTER ONE

THE GOOD NEWS

In medieval England, the town crier played a significant role by ringing a bell to announce the latest news, new laws, and royal proclamations. While some villagers undoubtedly ignored the crier, in wartime everyone paid attention to his announcements.

Imagine waking up each morning up eager to hear the herald's life-changing words. Did our soldiers secure victory or suffer defeat? Is my son a survivor or battle slain? Will we receive spoils of war or endure occupation? The herald's news could change just about everything.

IMPORTANT NEWS

The gospel—the message at the heart of the Christian faith—means "good news" or "good announcement." Like wartime declarations this announcement is urgent, but unlike the news of the town crier, this announcement truly changes everything. Consider what Saint Paul has to say about the good news.

In 1 Corinthians 15, Paul announces the good news concerning Jesus Christ:

> Now I would remind you, brothers [and sisters], of the gospel I preached to you... For I delivered to you as of first importance what I also received: that Christ died for our sins in accordance with the Scriptures, that he was buried, that he was raised on the third day in accordance with the Scriptures, and that he appeared to Cephas, then to the twelve. (15:1, 3–5)

This passage identifies several key things about the gospel. First, Paul insists he announced something of *first importance*. The word "first" can be ordinal, first in a series of things, or it can refer to rank, the most prominent of things. Paul is using

2

the latter meaning to indicate the foremost significance of the good news. It is an announcement about ultimate things. Through his birth, life, death, and resurrection Jesus has changed the course of history. The gospel is about someone truly and exclusively great, not dismissible news.

GOOD NEWS

But why is the gospel *good*? Paul bluntly writes, "If Christ has not been raised, your faith is futile and you are still in your sins" (1 Cor 15:17). The resurrection of Jesus secured his triumph over sin, death, and evil. Faith in a dead messiah is a foolish religion, but faith in a messiah who beat death changes everything. Jesus's triumph over sin, death, and evil secures many benefits, including the forgiveness of sins and hope of bodily resurrection. This is good news for those who sense their own brokenness and the fallenness of their own bodies. Jesus has done something decisive about our fractured world.

Paul continues, "But in fact Christ has been raised from the dead, the firstfruits of those who have fallen asleep" (1 Cor 15:20). How is Jesus the firstfruits of those who have fallen asleep, a euphemism for dying in Christ? In Judaism, the firstfruits were the part of the crop that was harvested first and set aside in dedication to God. Paul is saying that Jesus's resurrection is the first taste of a harvest of resurrections.

Those who hope in Jesus will receive resurrected bodies fit for a resurrected world! His victory wasn't only a triumph but a preview of things to come.

After viewing a trailer for the Christopher Nolan film, *Inception*, I couldn't wait for the film to release. I was so excited I shared it with others in anticipation of opening day. The gospel gives us a preview of Jesus transforming *everything*. It is an announcement that Jesus has put sin, death, and evil on notice *in his death*, and given us a sneak peek of a renewed creation *in his resurrection*. You see, when we put our faith in Christ, his death and resurrection are our death and resurrection, spiritually and physically. That's news worth sharing!

Reflection: *Think about an announcement that was so important to you that you couldn't hold it in. Why did that announcement rise to the top of your mind? Can you begin to see why the gospel is news worth believing and sharing?*

RECEIVED NEWS

Next, Paul indicates he delivered a gospel that he received: "Now I would remind you, brothers [and sisters], of the gospel I preached to you, which you received" (1 Cor 15:1). The Greek word here is translated "to hand down or receive." Paul uses the same word in Thessalonians when he mentions "the

4

tradition that you received" (2 Thess 3:6). What tradition is he referring to?

The tradition the churches received is not like the handed down practice of putting up a Christmas tree after Thanksgiving. Those cultural traditions come and go. The apostolic tradition is the divinely authorized gospel handed down to the church from the apostles who witnessed the risen Christ. This means the gospel is not only of first importance but also divinely authoritative. It is a message meant to order our lives.

The gospel is not just the ABCs but the A to Z of the Christian life.
—Tim Keller

Many messages order our lives. For example, we are often exhorted: "You do you." This message locates the authority for life decisions within ourselves. It implies that we should do whatever we *feel*, but the gospel message is rooted in what God says is true. Its authority exists outside of ourselves, providing a better vantage point from which to make decisions.

It comes as no surprise, then, when Paul commands the Thessalonians, "So then brothers [and sisters][1] *stand firm* and *hold to the traditions* that you were taught by us" (2 Thess 2:15). He knows that if we do not stand firm in what Christ has done for us, and what he is doing in the world, we will not experience the reliability of Christ.

Imagine summiting a mountain with a trusted friend. You notice a rocky ledge jutting out from the peak, and your friend climbs onto the ledge, a speck against the vast, green valley in the distance. Following suit, you scramble up the rocks and onto the ledge to join your friend. But as you move toward the edge, your legs begin to quiver; you feel skeptical the rock can hold you. Your friend cheers you on, assuring you the rock is reliable, but it isn't until you walk out onto the ledge that you discover just how strong the rock is. It is only by standing firm on the gospel that we discover just how strong and true it is.

DEALING WITH DOUBTS

In summary, the gospel is of first *importance*. It is ultimate news about what Jesus has accomplished for us, in his death and resurrection. The gospel is *good* news, not a forgettable announcement. The gospel is also *authoritative*. It is reliable

---

[1] In New Testament usage, depending on the context, the plural Greek word *adelphoi* (translated "brothers") may refer either to *brothers* or to *brothers* and *sisters*.

news we can stand on. All of these truths about the gospel are trustworthy and transformative, but that doesn't mean we don't have doubts.

What should we do when we have doubts about the gospel? When people share their doubts about Christianity, they often say something like, "I know I shouldn't doubt but ..." But their assumption isn't entirely true. What good are our beliefs if they can't stand up to our doubts?

Author Tim Keller notes, "A faith without some doubts is like a human body without any antibodies in it. People who blithely go through life too busy or indifferent to ask hard questions about why they believe as they do will find themselves defenseless against either the experience of tragedy or the probing questions of a smart skeptic."[2] Healthy skepticism builds up the faith.

In the mountain climbing story above, the rocky ledge holds whether or not a climber has the faith to stand on the ledge. In the same way, the gospel holds despite our doubts and reservations. No one is saved by the strength of their faith but by the object of their faith. Because the gospel holds firm through the accomplishments of Christ for us, we don't need to fear when doubt inevitably creeps in.

So bravely ask your questions but also be humble enough to welcome the answers. Question the reliability of the

---

[2] Timothy Keller, *The Reason for God: Belief in an Age of Skepticism* (New York: Dutton, 2010), xxiii.

gospel by putting your weight on the good news. Only then will you discover just how reliable the divine tradition is. Doubt not for doubt's sake, but to feel the firmness of the truth.

FOR FURTHER REFLECTION

Read and reflect *on the following passages, considering both the original author's intent and meaning, as well as the text's connection to the chapter's topic.*

1 Corinthians 15:1, 3-5   2 Thessalonians 2:15

Discussion questions

1. What are you hoping to get out of this book?

2. In your own words, what is the gospel and why is it so important? (You will be refining your answer throughout this book.)

3. Have you experienced doubts about the gospel, and if so, how have you handled them? What steps can you take to address your doubts in a healthy and constructive manner, without letting them weaken your faith?

4. Take a moment to assess your life. What is currently at the center of it, exerting the most influence? How can you actively place the gospel of Jesus at the center of your life and allow it to shape and direct everything else?

5. Have you ever felt bored when reading the Bible? How might patience and slowing down when reading actually help you appreciate the Bible better?

KEY PROJECT PREVIEW

Each Foundations book will include a key project, or two, to help you synthesize what you have learned. We encourage you to complete it by the time you finish the book, and then discuss it at your final group gathering.

There is one project for this book.

Written Personal Definition of the Gospel and Personal Testimony in Light of It

Write a definition of the gospel that is in your own words, but that also takes your learnings from the book into account. Additionally, write your personal testimony in such a way that it becomes a real-life demonstration of your personal definition of the gospel.

CHAPTER TWO

DEFINING
THE GOSPEL

If you were to write out a definition of the gospel, what things would you include? Would you include the death of Jesus but omit his resurrection? What about Jesus's life before the cross? Is that part of the gospel? Would you focus on the gospel's power to forgive sins but forget its power to renew all things? Our definitions of the gospel can either be too broad or too narrow.

DEFINING
THE GOSPEL

If you ask twenty Christians to define the gospel, you might get twenty different definitions. This is not because the gospel has multiple meanings but because it is multi-faceted. The gospel has an essential core—what Jesus has done for us through his life, death, and resurrection—and endless implications. Moreover, the Bible contains various images of salvation, reflecting significant unity and diversity in the way people define the gospel.

Take a look at these summary definitions of the gospel from a range of pastors and theologians:

"It is the good tidings that God has revealed concerning Christ."

"The message from our Lord Himself is that Christ suffered and was raised from the dead and that remission of sins should be preached in His name to all people."

"Gospel (from the Old English godspel, 'good tale') means 'good news,' and this is the best news there can be: in Jesus, the kingdom of God has come!"

"The gospel is the word about Jesus Christ and what he did for us in order to restore us to a right relationship with God."

"The gospel is the work of God to restore humans to union with God and communion with others, in the context of a community, for the good of others and the world."

Some of the different understandings of the gospel boil down to a matter of emphasis. Some believers emphasize the *personal* aspects of the gospel, while others emphasize the *cosmic* aspects of the gospel.

Many Christians have an LCD gospel, focusing on the lowest common denominator: Jesus died on the cross for my sins. While this is certainly true, it is an incomplete description of the gospel. It's a view of the gospel that focuses primarily on personal salvation—just give me the bare essentials and I'll believe.

Churches that focus on an LCD gospel often train people in evangelism, plant churches, and emphasize global missions, resulting in a tremendous spreading of the gospel. Their understanding of the seriousness of sin and the grace of God in Jesus compels them to share the good news. These churches also tend to promote serious Bible study and doctrinal conviction, helping to defend the Word of God from false gospels. While this focus is narrow, it is a critical part of the gospel.

However, the gospel also includes the life, resurrection, ascension, and return of Jesus. His work accounts not only for how *we* are reconciled to God but how *all things* are reconciled to God: "... and through him to reconcile to himself all things, whether on earth or in heaven, making peace by the blood of his cross" (Col 1:20). More than an LCD version, the gospel is a TOE version: a theory of everything. This accounts for how the whole cosmos hangs together and how all things will be made new.

Churches that focus on the TOE gospel often promote the arts and pursue social justice. Their understanding of the creation mandate given to Adam and Eve, and the promise of a beautiful, urban new creation, motivates creativity for the glory of God. Churches that grasp the just, multiethnic future of the new creation, tend to do a better job at cultivating diverse and just communities. While this focus is broad, it is an important aspect of the gospel.

Some of us lean toward a narrow, LCD gospel. Others lean toward a broad, TOE gospel. Those who focus on the LCD gospel tend to be more attentive to evangelism, Bible study, and doctrine. Those who focus on the TOE gospel are often more concerned about social justice, community, and counseling.

It is important to note that some believe the gospel is narrower in its definition but deep and broad in its application—a combination of the LCD and TOE views.

THE GOSPEL PLOTLINE

Another way to grasp the gospel is to recognize the good news as a story. The narrative of the gospel has been unfolding along a basic plotline from the beginning of Genesis: creation–fall–redemption–new creation.

Creation

In creation, God created a world to reflect his truth, beauty, and goodness. He created humanity in his own image to rule over and fill creation with his glorious image, resulting in thriving communities and diverse cultures (Gen 1:26–28).

Fall

In the garden of Eden, Adam and Eve rejected God's design for creation and distorted the image of God. Humanity multiplied as a marred, self-centered image. As a result, the communities and cultures that followed fell into glorious ruin, both beautiful and broken, requiring redemption. Before expelling Adam and Eve from the garden, God promised to send a Redeemer into the world (Gen 3:15).

Redemption

After Adam and Eve's failure, God called out a new people to spread his glorious image, Israel. However, like Adam, Israel also rebelled against God and was exiled from their land (2

Chr 36:17–21; Jer 16:13). Yet, again, God promised to send a Redeemer who would rescue his people from exile and redeem the nations (Jer 16:14–15; 31:10–14). Jesus became the better Israel and truer Adam. Through his life, death, and resurrection, he secured redemption for his people and all creation.

New Creation

Jesus's first coming inaugurated a redemption that is not yet consummated. We are already redeemed people (Eph 1:7) who have not yet reached the final day of redemption (Eph 4:30). We are new creatures who long for a new creation. When Jesus returns, he will renovate the cosmos by making it a place where we dwell in peace and righteousness in a new heavens and earth (Rev 21:1–4).

———————

This sweeping, redemptive narrative is often broken up. Some lop off the bookends of the gospel story. Removing creation and new creation, they focus on sin and salvation. Other Christians cut out the middle of the story, removing fall and redemption. As a result, they focus on creativity and justice.

But the gospel is a whole story for the whole world. It is good news not only for all creation but for individual creatures. The gospel is as big as the cosmos and as small as you and me.

A GOSPEL DEFINITION

Here is a definition of the good news that captures both its narrow and broad contours:

> The gospel is the good and true story that Jesus has defeated sin, death, and evil through his own life, death, and resurrection and is making all things new, even us.

This definition of the gospel contains four primary aspects: historical, doctrinal, personal, and cosmic.

Historical Gospel

First, the gospel is *historical*. Paul's announcement in 1 Corinthians 15 is not a set of doctrines abstracted from history. Rather, it is rooted in events that took place in space and time. These events were recorded, witnessed, and experienced by first-century people.

Paul notes that Jesus's death, burial, and resurrection were "according to the Scriptures" (vv. 3, 4). It was predicted and recorded in both the Old and New Testaments and appealed to eyewitness testimony of Jesus's resurrection: "Then he appeared to more than five hundred brothers at one time, most of whom are still alive" (v. 6). Paul also gives personal testimony to his encounter with the risen Christ: "Last of all, as to one untimely born, he appeared also to me" (v. 8). This encounter permanently altered Paul's life, transforming him from persecutor of the church to protector of its gospel (v. 11).

Some faiths are not rooted in historical events, providing them with little foundational support. Buddhism is based on the philosophical musings of the Buddha, which he codified into the Four Noble Truths and the eightfold Noble Path. Rhonda Byrne, author of the bestselling spiritual, *The Secret*, says the key to spiritual happiness is getting in tune with the universe by receiving its frequencies into our minds. Yet, there is no historical or scientific evidence that an impersonal universe can communicate with personal beings. Expressive individualism—the belief that meaning and purpose comes from self-expression—insists that an individual's core feelings should determine what is good.

Reflection: *Think of some Eastern religions or Western spiritualities that are untethered to history. How is Christianity distinct from these faiths?*

Unlike the philosophical abstractions of Buddha, or the psychological tenets of expressive individualism, Christianity is a verifiable story. The life and ministry of Jesus is widely documented in the Gospels and other literature. It is also "according to the Scriptures," meaning the story stretches back thousands of years into the Old Testament. The gospel is God's salvific plan for a world gone wrong. It is a good and true story.

Doctrinal Gospel

The gospel is also *doctrinal*: it is meant to define what we believe. While the good news has a narrative shape, the New Testament epistles are filled with doctrinal reflection on the gospel. The gospel makes claims about the nature of humanity, the person of Christ, how we are reconciled to God, and his plan for the world. It isn't a fictional tale but a story with firm beliefs.

THE ATONEMENT

There are many rich doctrinal elements to the gospel, five of which we will examine in chapter 4. For now, we will focus on the atonement by reflecting on what John Piper has called the most important paragraph in the Bible, Romans 3.

> But now the righteousness of God has been manifested apart from the law, although the Law and the Prophets bear witness to it—the righteousness of God through faith in Jesus Christ for all who believe. For there is no distinction: for fall have sinned and fall short of the glory of God, and are justified by his grace as a gift, through the redemption that is in Christ Jesus, whom God put forward as a propitiation by his blood, to be received by

faith. This was to show God's righteousness, because in his divine forbearance he had passed over former sins. It was to show his righteousness at the present time, so that he might be just and the justifier of the one who has faith in Jesus. (Rom 3:21–26)

In this passage, Paul argues that we are justified "through the redemption that is in Christ Jesus, whom God put forward as a propitiation by his blood" (vv. 24–25). Both the NIV and the NRSV translate the word "propitiation" as "atonement." What is "atonement"? Atonement is the sacrificial, wrath-bearing, substitutionary death of Jesus for sinners to lovingly reconcile them to God.

The notion of a sacrificial, substitutionary death can sound archaic and crude to modern people. In fact, people often say it is this aspect of Christianity they find most offensive, comparing it to child sacrifice. It conjures up images from Greek mythology, like Agamemnon, who beset by winds couldn't launch his fleet until he sacrificed his daughter to the goddess Artemis. Is the God of the Bible acting like Artemis?

The word atonement draws on an Anglo-Saxon word that means "making at one." This refers to the act of bringing two estranged parties together. In Leviticus 23, atonement law required the death of an unblemished, perfect animal

20

to bring man back into fellowship with God. A death was required to atone for the crime perpetrated by the sinner.

However, for atonement to occur, the punishment must fit the crime. For this reason, Paul says, "In [God's] divine forbearance he had passed over former sins" (Rom 3:25). Animals were an inadequate sacrifice for sins: "For it is impossible for the blood of bulls and goats to take away sins (Heb 10:4). Even in Levitical law, the punishment did not fit the crime, nor could it make perfect those who drew near in worship. Then what punishment does fit the crime of our sins against God?

Imagine you are in a car wreck and someone totals your car, but their insurance is only willing to pay a fraction of its value. Would you shrug it off? No, you would insist the payout of the insurance company be commensurate to the value of your car. We get angry when the punishment does not fit the crime; we feel it is unfair. Now, apply that principle to the damage done to God's infinite glory for refusing to honor him. We've done way worse than totaling a Toyota. We've made a wreck of his infinite glory (Rom 3:23). God's wrath is not an off-the-cuff, wild anger; it is his perfect, controlled, and good response to sin.

Fortunately, God does not require us to sacrifice our most fit child. That would wrongly punish the innocent for the guilty. *Our* wages of sin warrant *our* death (Rom 6:23). But in a stunning act of mercy, the offended party sacrifices himself. On the cross, the infinite Son of God absorbs the cost of our offense against an infinite God. Jesus pays for the damage we have done to God's glory.

This is the total opposite of Greek thinking. In Christianity, God does not require anyone to sacrifice a son or daughter, but instead, he offers his own infinite, perfect Son "as a propitiation in his blood" so we don't have to die. Jesus does our time on his cross. He suffers the wages of death so we can truly live "at one" with God. Jesus paid it all.

Now, some object to the atonement by asking how a loving God could pour out wrath on his own Son. They decry it as divine child abuse. But the cross was not something that took Jesus by surprise. Rather, it was a cost he agreed to with the Father and willingly absorbed on our behalf (Heb 7:20–22; John 17). On the cross, we witness the Judge who himself willingly underwent judgment.

> ## "God does not love us because Christ died for us; Christ died for us because God loved us." —John Stott

The atonement is the opposite of abuse. First John 4:8 is frequently cited in support of the idea that "God is love." But how exactly does God express his love? The next two verses explain: "In this is love, not that we have loved God but that he loved us and sent his Son to be the propitiation for our sins" (1 John 4:10). How do we know God is love? Because he gave up his only Son to endure a sacrificial, wrath-bearing death for our sins. Far from abuse, this is love.

Jesus's atonement is a momentous expression of mercy that calls forth a fountain of faith. Through this act he invites us to spend our days cherishing his sacrificial, substitutionary death in living a life free from guilt and condemnation.

THE VICTORY OF CHRIST

While the atonement is propitiatory, it is also victorious. If we're not attentive to the gospel, we may receive the gift of Jesus's atoning work for past sins but fail to enjoy his victory over future sins. Remember, the gospel is the good and true story that Jesus has defeated sin, death, and evil. Let's consider the greatness of Christ's victory.

A cursory reading of 1 Corinthians 15 reveals that Jesus triumphed over sin, death, and evil:

- "Died for our sins" (v. 4)
- "The last enemy to be destroyed is death" (v. 26)
- "Destroying every rule and every authority and power" (v. 24)

Jesus defeated the penalty of our sin, the power of death, and the presence of evil. Sin is forgiven through Jesus's substitutionary death in our place. Death is subverted by his resurrection life, which will eventually manifest into resurrection bodies for all who hope in him. Evil is cut off at the source, and put on notice, because Jesus promises to destroy every sinister authority. This triumph is news the world so desperately wants: victory over sin, death, and evil!

Jesus's victory was subversive. He did not wave a wand over the cosmos and say, "Forgiven!" Rather, as the second Adam, Jesus entered into history to undo the damage of the first Adam. What Adam courted in the garden of Eden, Jesus conquered in the garden of Golgotha (John 19:41). The cost of victory was the loss of his very own life.

This is offensive news to self-important people. It means we are so bad that we need the infinitely good and perfect Christ to die on our behalf, which he did freely. Jesus lovingly confers on us an importance we could never create ourselves. The gospel imbues us with incredible worth: the Son of God threw himself on the tracks for us. It also assures us that death will be no more: Jesus rose from the dead. It secures total triumph over Satan and his powers, "through the resurrection of Jesus Christ, who has gone into heaven and is at the right hand of God, with angels, authorities, and powers having been subjected to him (1 Pet 3:21–22). Jesus will destroy every power.

But how can this triumph affect our daily lives? If we embrace the victory of Christ, we will live in power over sin: "His divine power has granted to us all things that pertain to life and godliness" (2 Pet 1:3). The power that conquered sin, death, and hell flows through us. Jesus does not withhold his strength but imparts to us all things for a godly life.

Paul reminds us that we are more than conquerors in Christ (Rom 8:37–39). The word for "more than conquerors" is a compound word that means hyper-victorious. We participate fully in the victory of Christ. No power has a claim on us, and even though we falter, nothing can separate us from the love of God:

> For I am sure that neither death nor life, nor angels nor rulers, nor things present nor things to come, nor powers, nor height nor depth, nor anything else in all creation, will be able to separate us from the love of God in Christ Jesus our Lord. (Rom 8:38–39)

The victory of Christ produces full-orbed holiness. Conservatives tend to emphasize Jesus's triumph over sin but neglect his victory over evil, emphasizing personal holiness to the exclusion of social holiness. Yet they have a strength in focusing on sexual purity, church participation, and personal evangelism.

Progressives tend to emphasize Jesus's victory over evil while minimizing the need for repentance from personal sin. They have a commendable focus on social holiness: the poor, systemic racism, and environmental action.

May the Lord make us humble enough to learn from one another to practice full-orbed holiness by participating in the victory of Christ over the powers.

Reflection: *How can you claim the victory of Christ more fully in your life?*

Personal Gospel

While the gospel changes what we believe, believing its truths also transforms us. The gospel is *personal*: it changes who we are. This is generally true about any of our beliefs. If we believe a belittling narrative from our family of origin, it malforms our identity: "You're a loser and will never amount to anything." Believing this lie can have catastrophic effects on our self-worth and relationships.

Alternatively, when we believe the truth of the gospel, it reshapes our identity: "In love he predestined us for adoption to himself as sons through Jesus Christ" (Eph 1:4–5). Cherishing this truth transforms our self-worth and the way we relate to others. When I believe that God the Father adopted me into his family through Jesus, I enjoy an adoptive love that frees me from condemning narratives. My worth is no longer rooted in how I perform but who I am—son or daughter of God.

Cosmic Gospel

The gospel is also *cosmic*: it changes where we live. This is reflected in the words of the gospel definition given earlier: "God is making all things new, even us." This cosmos-altering aspect of the gospel is embedded in 1 Corinthians 15 when Paul writes that all things will be subjected to God that God may be all in all (v. 28). When Jesus finishes putting all his enemies under his feet, he will hand over the cosmos to God for its final and full reordering. Sin, death, and evil will be no more. Everything will be suffused with the redeeming, restorative grace of God such that God will be all in all. Nothing will be godless; all will be ruled by the goodness of the triune God.

If you were to ask a stranger what they hope the future will be like, they might describe a world without war, poverty, and injustice. A place of peace, plenty, equality, justice, and joy. Without knowing it, they would be describing the future promised to those who are in Christ—a new heavens and earth. This is the world we all want, and in Christ, it is the world that has already begun.

After his forty-day temptation in the wilderness, Jesus returned to Galilee, entered a synagogue, and preached the gospel for the first time. He was handed the scroll of Isaiah to read aloud:

The Spirit of the Lord is upon me,
because he has anointed me
to proclaim good news to the poor.
He has sent me to proclaim liberty to the captives
and recovering of sight to the blind,
to set at liberty those who are oppressed,
to proclaim the year of the Lord's favor.
(Luke 4:18–19; Isa 61:1–2)

With the eyes of his audience transfixed on him, Jesus gave an inspired commentary on this passage, "Today this Scripture has been fulfilled in your hearing" (Luke 4:21). With this incredible claim, Jesus inaugurated the favorable year of the Lord, an age in which the peace, justice, mercy, and joy of the future are brought into the present.

We read about the devastating effects of the fall in our newsfeeds every day. It is also documented on virtually every page of the Bible. Creation groans, awaiting the consummation of Christ's work (Rom 8:22–23). Yet the Bible not only explains and validates the problem of evil, it provides the only solution—the Spirit-anointed, captive-releasing, cosmos-restoring Messiah. Therefore, we ought to spread this news like it is truly good.

Isaiah 61 contains a vivid depiction of all things new. City walls are repaired, prisoners are set free, the lame are healed, and the nations stream to Zion bringing cultural tribute to God.

———————

In summary, the gospel is *historical*: it is rooted in space and time; it is *doctrinal*: it changes what we believe; it is *personal*: it changes who we are; and it is *cosmic* or missional: it changes where we live. These four aspects of the gospel reveal some of the complexity, beauty, and depth of the good news. With the stunning plotline of creation-fall-redemption-new creation, let's not lop off the ends of the story or cut out the middle but honor the whole gospel story.

FOR FURTHER REFLECTION

Read and reflect *on the following passages, considering both the original author's intent and meaning, as well as the text's connection to the chapter's topic.*

  2 Corinthians 5:19-21   Colossians 1:20   Romans 3:21-26

Discussion questions

1. After reading this chapter, how would you now personally define the gospel?

2. Reflect on the various definitions of the gospel mentioned in the chapter, such as the LCD gospel and the TOE gospel. Which definition resonates with you the most, and why?

3. What must be part of a gospel definition regardless of being more narrow or broad? What is the danger of having an imbalanced view of the gospel?

4. Consider the cosmic aspect of the gospel and the vision of a new heavens and earth where God's justice and goodness reign. How does this future hope impact our present reality? How could it equip you to talk with non-Christians?

CHAPTER THREE

RESPONDING TO THE GOSPEL

Since the gospel is an announcement that comes on good authority, it demands a response. It is not simply enough to hear the story or agree with its facts. Upon hearing the gospel, we are called to respond.

> Now after John was arrested, Jesus came into Galilee, proclaiming the gospel of God, and saying, "The time is fulfilled, and the kingdom of God is at hand; repent and believe in the gospel." (Mark 1:14–15)

When Jesus preached the gospel of God, he preached himself. He is the good news. Israel's king had finally come; his kingdom was at hand. What response does king Jesus demand? Repent and believe in the gospel.

When we hear "repent and believe" with modern ears, we may assume it means to quit sinning (repent) and do better (believe). But this is not what Jesus intended.

REPENTANCE

The word repent means "to turn away," not simply from sin but from its false promises. While Jesus called for initial repentance for salvation, repentance is also a necessary part of our sanctification. In salvation we are reconciled to God through faith in Jesus. Sanctification is the outworking of our salvation, a process of being transformed into the likeness of Christ through repentance and faith in the gospel.

Our initial repentance is like a marital vow made on a wedding day to form a covenant with a spouse. Continual repentance does not replace that initial act but builds upon it, like returning to a marital covenant reminds us to live out our vows faithfully in union with our spouse.

Scripture identifies the importance of continual repentance when Jesus calls five of the seven churches of Revelation 2–3 to repent: "Remember therefore from where you have fallen; repent, and do the works you did at first. If not, I will come to you and remove your lampstand from its place, unless you repent" (Rev 2:5; see also 2:16, 21; 3:3, 19). Repentance is an all-of-life endeavor.

Let's consider an example of continual repentance. When we lust after someone, we express faith in what we think a person can do for us. Entertaining a sexual fantasy of a passerby, we may believe they can give us satisfaction. Viewing pornography in demanding seasons, we may believe the distraction will bring relief from stress and give us peace. But lust never keeps its promises.

To repent of lust, we must turn from trusting in the false promises of lust to trusting in the true promises of Jesus. Christ teaches, "Blessed are those who hunger and thirst for righteousness, for they shall be satisfied" (Matt 5:6). True satisfaction comes from feasting on Christ and his righteousness, not other people. Jesus also says, "Peace I leave with you; my peace I give to you. Not as the world gives do I give to you. Let not your hearts be troubled, neither let them be afraid" (Jn 14:27). Real relief from stress comes, not from worldly distraction, but by entrusting our anxiety to Jesus, who gives us his peace.

To repent, we must turn away from false promises to face Jesus and trust his promises. This single motion of faith is an act of faith in Jesus's forgiving grace and trustworthy truths. When we repent, we get more of Jesus!

However, repentance can be a confusing concept. It's so easy to get off track in following Jesus. Let's consider a few pitfalls of repentance in order to enjoy more of Jesus

Self-Atoning Penance

Unfortunately, repentance often conjures up negative images for people like groveling or self-flagellation. It's easy to view our need for repentance as being on God's bad side and feeling bitterly about ourselves until we get back on his good side. However, this view of repentance has more in common with penance—the Roman Catholic concept of amending ourselves to make atonement.

The *Catechism of the Catholic Church* says, "The sinner must still recover his full spiritual health by doing something more to make amends for the sin: he must 'make satisfaction for' or 'expiate' his sins."[1] This places part of the weight of making atonement on the sinner, but in the gospel, Jesus alone makes amends for our sins so we can enjoy spiritual life and peace.

Like a chair forced to hold a weight it can't bear, people break when they believe the lie of self-penance. Usually the breaking point is despair—our souls crushed under the constant weight of wondering, *Have I really been good enough to get back into God's favor?* Or we suffer from spiritual pride,

---

[1] Catholic Church, *Catechism of the Catholic Church*, 2nd ed. (Our Sunday Visitor, 2000), 1459. https://www.vatican.va/archive/ENG0015/_P4D.HTM

our souls falsely inflated with arrogance when we think, *I'm doing good and so much better than "those people."* Both errors come from trusting in ourselves rather than repenting of our sins and repenting of our attempts to earn God's love.

Hasty Repentance

Alternatively, we may practice what Christian philosopher Soren Kierkegaard describes as "sudden" or "hasty repentance." He describes this as an impulse "to collect all the sorrow of sin in one draft" and be done with it. It is an attempt to get away from guilt without getting close to Christ. We might repent hastily by tossing up a silent, "Forgive me, Lord," without any remorse. Or we may confess our sin to a friend without even addressing the Lord. In sudden repentance we seek to clear our conscience but not encounter Christ. As a result, we miss out on the joy of forgiveness, the possibility of transformation, and the hope of the gospel. How, then, should we practice hopeful, gospel-centered repentance?

Slow Repentance

Kierkegaard writes, "It is indeed true that guilt must stand vividly before a person if he is truly to repent."[2] For guilt to become vivid, we need time to contemplate our sins before

---

[2] Soren Kierkegaard, "On the Occasion of a Confession" in *Upbuilding Discourses in Various Spirits*, ed. and trans. Howard V. Hong and Edna H. Hong, Kierkegaard's Writings 15 (Princeton, NJ: Princeton University Press, 1993), 17.

the Lord: "Search me, O God, and know my heart! Try me and know my thoughts! And see if there be any grievous way in me, and lead me in the way everlasting" (Ps 139:23–24). The key is to include Christ in our humble confession. As we do, genuine contrition ripens in our hearts. Slow repentance can be much more life-giving.

Slow repentance also enables the object of our repentance to become clear to us. Instead of just confessing our sin, we will inquire of the Lord for help. This may include prayers like, "Lord, help me discern what is motivating my anger and help me turn away from it to Jesus." Or, "Lord, I confess I have sought acceptance from others in gossip instead of enjoying your acceptance in Christ." The point of slow repentance is not length of time but genuineness of turning to Christ. Pinpointing our reason for sinning helps us turn to him.

Paul writes to the Corinthians, "For godly grief produces a repentance that leads to salvation without regret, whereas worldly grief produces death" (2 Cor 7:10). Godly sorrow helps us recognize our guilt and repent of sin in sincere, hopeful confession. Returning to Revelation, we observe Jesus's motivation in calling us to repent: "Those whom I love, I reprove and discipline, so be zealous and repent" (Rev 3:19). It is out of his boundless love that Jesus calls us to be zealous and repent.

Worldly sorrow, like hasty repentance, is only concerned with appearances. Godly sorrow helps us recognize our guilt and repent of sin in sincere, hopeful confession, believing there is more grace in Christ than sin in us.

Dan was an accomplished cellist and deep thinker. After we met, we started connecting at a pub every few weeks to discuss his objections to Christianity. Eventually he asked me, "Do you ever doubt your faith?" I paused and thought for a moment. Then I responded, "After decades of study and following Jesus, I don't really doubt as much as I disbelieve." He looked at me quizzically, "What's the difference?"

Well, earlier today I posted something on social media that I thought was insightful and checked back to see if anyone liked it. Nothing, so I decided to check back later. Still nothing, no heart, no retweet, no comment, and my heart sank. In that moment, I believed the approval of anonymous internet users was better than the approval of God in Christ. I disbelieved the gospel.

While I believed facts *about* gospel, I lacked faith in the gospel. So I repented of trusting in anonymous approval by turning to the Father's perfect approval in Christ. Lord, forgive me for cherishing worldy approval that makes much of me, and help me trust in eternal approval that comes from you." as I shared my repentance with him, Dan's countenance changed. Suddenly the gospel made sense to him. My act of continual repentance led to his initial act of repentance.

When I was convicted of prizing the approval of social media over the approval of God the Father, I confessed my sin to him and asked him to ravish my heart with his approval. I admitted my sin to God, not just to myself. I pinpointed what was driving my sin as best as I could (approval of man) and included Jesus by asking him to help me enjoy his approval more. The subsequent experience of his healing forgiveness and genuine love freed me to admit my sin to my friend, which God used to open his eyes to God's grace. Through repentance, both myself and my friend were drawn to see the beauty and power of Jesus. This is why repentance is always a joyous thing—it's a return home to the open arms of the Father who loves us (Luke 15:1–7).

Reflection: *Do you practice slow repentance? Do you have a regular rhythm of reflecting on your sins and returning to the Savior? If yes, what does that look like? If not, why not?*

BELIEF

Jesus not only called people to repent but also to believe. What is belief? Belief is heartfelt trust in the promises of God. Jesus isn't merely asking us to agree that he is better than all other things (even demons believe that) but to cherish him as best, chief, Lord and Savior of all. What, then, does repentance and belief look like?

Repentance and belief are not a two-step process: we repent and Jesus meets us halfway with belief. No, repentance and belief are the double-sided coin of response to the good news: a single motion motivated by grace. If I am standing and staring at one wall, in order to face the opposing wall, I must turn one hundred and eighty degrees. There is no half-turn to face Jesus. To turn away from the fleeting promises of sin, I turn around to face the welcoming, forgiving presence of our Savior.

In Peter Jackson's film adaptation of J. R. R. Tolkien's novel, *The Hobbit*, there is a scene where Bilbo, the dwarfs, and Gandalf are trapped in the trees at the edge of a cliff. With fires blazing beneath them, the heroes have no hope of escape. The evil white orc and his minions barrel down upon them, snapping tree limbs, and send the protagonists dangling over the cliff. Just before tumbling to their deaths, Bilbo exclaims, "The eagles! The eagles are coming!" The great eagles called by Gandalf suddenly swoop down and rescue them.

At that moment, viewers are struck by a simultaneous feeling of desperation and joy. This turn from sadness to joy is what Tolkien calls the *eucatastrophe* (a good catastrophe). His novels are filled with these moments, which he describes as "the sudden happy turn in a story, which pierces you with a joy that brings tears."[3] It is the moment when the story reaches through the pages, grasps your beating heart, and seizes your longings.

The eucatastrophe, Tolkien says, is the gospel of Jesus. It is not an awe-inspiring fictional feeling but the sudden, happy turn of humanity from sadness to joy. It is a picture of repentance, a turn from the sadness of sin to the joy of knowing Jesus Christ. While the intensity of our sadness and joy will wax and wane, the reliability of God's rescuing love does not. Christ is eager to receive and rescue us, every single time. Remember the example of the rocky ledge in chapter 1? What matters most is not the strength of our faith but the object of our faith. Christ is a firm, solid ledge. Our faith matters, but it is the solid rock on which we stand—even as our faith wavers—that saves us at the moment of our great need, leading to great joy.

---

[3] J. R. R. Tolkien, *The Letters of J. R. R. Tolkien*, "To Christopher Tolkien," November 7–8, 1944 (FS 60), 20 Northmoor Road, Oxford.

FOR FURTHER REFLECTION

Read and reflect *on the following passages, considering both the original author's intent and meaning, as well as the text's connection to the chapter's topic.*

Mark 1:14-15   Acts 2:37-38   2 Corinthians 7:10

Discussion questions

1. What is repentance? How do false repentance and true repentance differ?

2. What is belief? What is the connection between repentance and belief?

3. What is the difference between our initial repentance for salvation and our ongoing repentance once we're saved?

4. We are saved by the object, not the quality of our faith. How might this comfort you or someone who struggles to believe?

CHAPTER 4

GOSPEL
METAPHORS

While we have covered four aspects of the gospel, there is more depth to the good news. It is more doctrinally rich and personally transformative than we might imagine. The Scriptures express the gospel through a variety of metaphors that stretch across the breadth of the Bible and coalesce in the epistles.[1]

Metaphors might feel out of place in a discussion on the gospel, but they are God's way of using true images to cap-

---

[1] These metaphors are explained and applied for evangelism in Jonathan K. Dodson, *The Unbelievable Gospel: Say Something Worth Believing* (Grand Rapids, MI: Zondervan, 2014), 127–89.

ture different angles on the inexhaustible grace given to us in Jesus. In the epistles, these metaphors appear in five distinct categories: redemption, justification, adoption, new creation, and union with Christ. Like facets of a diamond, each of these metaphors convey a glorious theological truth about the historic work of Christ. Let's slowly turn the diamond and take a closer look at each of these gospel metaphors.

REDEMPTION

The gospel of redemption is a sacrificial metaphor that addresses our state of slavery to sin and consequent guilt. Since we cannot free ourselves from sin, we need someone to redeem us, which means "to set loose." The price for our freedom is death, so Jesus graciously sacrifices himself to pay our debt and set us free: "In him we have redemption through his blood, the forgiveness of our trespasses, according to the riches of his grace" (Eph 1:7). Jesus died the death we could not die to give us a life we could never live. As a result, we are freed and forgiven from sin.

The Quiet Place is a post-apocalyptic, science-fiction film about the Abbott family trying to survive in a world where aliens destroy anything that makes noise. The Abbots must move deftly and quietly through life to avoid death. In one scene, Reagan, the deaf daughter of Evelyn and Lee Abbot, gets frustrated with her father, pulls out her hearing aid, and wanders off. Meanwhile, a monster attacks their home. When she returns, she looks up to see a monster hanging over her. In the distance her father mouths to her, "I love you," just before making a noise to attract the monster to kill him instead of her. His death allows Reagan to escape.

Similarly, we have stormed off in sin from the love of our heavenly Father. With monstrous guilt bearing down upon us, Jesus called the Father's wrath upon himself in order to redeem us. Like Lee Abbott, Jesus gave up his life to rescue us from sin while mouthing from the cross, "I love you."

JUSTIFICATION

The gospel of justification is a legal metaphor that resolves the dilemma of how a righteous God can relate to unrighteous people and still remain righteous. The solution is found in Jesus "fulfilling all righteousness" (Matt 3:15) on our behalf by living a perfect life, dying in our place, and rising from the dead to draw us into his spotless righteousness: "Yet we know that a person is not justified by works of the law but through faith in Jesus Christ" (Gal 2:16).

Imagine standing before a judge ready to receive a life sentence for your crime. Before delivering the verdict, the judge takes off his robe and takes your place. When the verdict is passed, he agrees to do your time and places his robe upon you. You are declared innocent and set free. This is a picture of justification: Christ's substitutionary death upholds justice, and his innocent, righteous life is conferred upon you. As a result, you are set free.[2]

Although we could never do enough works to be accepted by God, Christ has done more than enough to make us eternally acceptable. Therefore, when we put our faith in Jesus, God looks at us as if we had done what Christ has done. As a result, we are fully accepted by God.

ADOPTION

The gospel of adoption is a familial metaphor that changes our status before God. Jesus rescues us out of Satan's family as "children of wrath" (Eph 2:3) to relocate us into the Father's family as "children of God" (1 John 3:1). In Jesus, enemies of God are made not only friends but family: "In Christ Jesus you are all sons of God, through faith" (Gal 3:26). Jesus changes not only our legal status but our family position. As a result, we enjoy God's approving love as his children.

My good friends applied to adopt a child from Africa. When they were finally approved, they traveled to Ethiopia to meet their three-year-old daughter. Abandoned by her parents, she was living in a tawdry orphanage. But out of their great love, her new parents welcomed her into their

---

[2] This illustration is used in J. I. Packer's *Knowing God* (Downers Grove, IL: IVP, 1973).

family, gave her their name, and provided her with every-thing she needed. A small group of us stood at the bottom of the airport escalator waiting for them to return from Ethiopia. When they appeared on the escalator with their new daughter in their arms, we all erupted in celebration.

> "Adoption is the highest privilege of the gospel. The traitor is forgiven, brought in for supper, and given the family name. To be right with God the Judge is a great thing, but to be loved and cared for by God the Father is greater." —J. I. PACKER

Similarly, we are conceived in iniquity and born to a father who does not want us. But out of his great love, God rescues us in Christ, welcomes us into his family, and gives us his name, providing everything we need. Like the return of the prodigal son, all of heaven throws a party to celebrate when one sinner repents, recognizing that we belong in God's family forever (Luke 15:22–24).

NEW CREATION

If justification changes our legal standing and adoption changes our familial status, then the gospel of new creation changes our spiritual nature. Although we are naturally "dead in our trespasses," God makes us supernaturally "alive together with Christ" (Eph 2:5). This new life is the eternal life imparted by the Spirit through the resurrected Christ, also referred to as "regeneration" (Titus 3:5). In Jesus, our old life is exiled and a new life takes its place. As a result, we gain a new identity and power to live with Christ.

When I met John, he was in a rehab facility recovering from an addiction to meth. We sat down at a cracked concrete table, and I said, "I imagine this isn't what you dreamed of when you were a kid. Tell me how you got here." John told me how he was given up for adoption as a kid, experienced rejection in school, and started using drugs to cope. As I looked across the table at this broken, bloated, and disheveled man, I asked him if he wanted to be a new man. He replied, "I guess."

I explained that Jesus died and rose to exile the old man and to make him a new man. After discipling him for several years, John got his teeth fixed, lost weight, and put his faith in Jesus. Then one Sunday he stood up and kicked the doors off his addiction, sharing with our church how God had saved him and made him a new creation. While not everyone's story of conversion will have such dramatic, immediate, or visible changes like John's, the truth is that all who trust in Christ are indeed a new creation.

UNION WITH CHRIST

Union with Christ is the glowing heart of the gospel diamond. It refers to intimate, mystical hiddenness in Jesus: "For you have died, and your life is hidden with Christ in God" (Col 3:3). This means that our very existence is now tucked away in Jesus, beyond the reach of anything or anyone. We are eternally his, and he is God's, making us doubly secure.

How is this wonderful, mystical union made possible? Referring to the work of the Holy Spirit, Jesus says, "In that day you will know that I am in my Father, and you in me, and I in you" (John 14:20). Through the Spirit, we are in Christ and Christ is in us. This mutual indwelling inseparably unites us to Jesus, fostering soul-satisfying communion with God.

The New Testament refers to this union 164 times, using the shorthand "in Christ." In Ephesians 1, various gospel metaphors are conveyed to us in Christ. Here are a few:

- "... *blessed* us in Christ with every spiritual blessing" (v. 3)

- "... *chose us* in him" (v. 4)

- "*Adoption* to himself as sons through Christ" (v. 5)

- "In him we have *redemption* through his blood" (v. 7)

- "In him we have obtained an *inheritance*" (v. 11)

The blessings of being chosen, adopted, redeemed, and an heir are all conveyed to us in Christ. If we are not united with Christ, we cannot receive any gospel benefits. But in Christ, we gain the world (1 Cor 3:22). As the glowing heart of the diamond, union with Christ pulls all other facets of the gospel in around us, enveloping us with his grace. Hidden inside the heart of Christ, we are perfectly and fully loved.

All analogies fall short in describing our mystical, intimate union with Jesus. Yet Scripture uses the image of a building and its cornerstone to convey our dependence upon Christ, a vine and its branches to convey our vital life in Christ, and the union between husband and wife to communicate the mysterious union and love of Christ with us.

Picking up on the latter, we could say that union with Christ is akin to an impoverished woman being chosen and loved by a billionaire who shares everything he has, and all that he is, with her. Now she, too, is a billionaire, but more importantly, she is a wife, one with her husband. Everything that Christ has, we have. And like this woman, we now exist as one with our new husband, bearing not only his benefits but his very name.

GOSPEL BENEFITS

As we turned the gospel diamond, I hope you have been stunned by the beauty of what Jesus has accomplished for you. Each metaphor conveys a unique benefit to those who are in Christ.

COSMIC GOSPEL

Interestingly, each of these metaphors also has cosmic significance. As the agent of creation and redemption, Jesus died and rose to make all things new.

Redemption: The world is *reconciled* to God through the blood of the cross (Col 1:20).

Justification: The new heavens and earth are where *righteousness* dwells (2 Pet 3:13).

Adoption: The adoption of the sons of God triggers the healing of all creation (Rom 8:18–25).

New Creation: The whole world will be regenerated into a new creation (Matt 19:28; Rev 21)

Union with Christ: All things will be summed up in Christ (Eph 1:11).

Reflecting on these five gospel metaphors, I hope you've grasped that the gospel truly is as big as the cosmos and as small as you and me.

FOR FURTHER REFLECTION

Read and reflect *on the following passages, considering both the original author's intent and meaning, as well as the text's connection to the chapter's topic.*

Ephesians 1:7   Galatians 2:16   Galatians 3:26   Colossians 3:3

Discussion questions

1. Of all the metaphors the Bible uses to talk about the Gospel, or the implications of the Gospel, what resonates with you most? Why?

2. Why is union with Christ such a big deal? How can or should it impact your daily life?

3. How might you share the Gospel with someone using the various metaphors from this chapter?

CHAPTER 5

ANOTHER GOSPEL

One of the keys to enjoying the gospel is to distinguish it from false gospels. Paul writes to the Galatian Christians, "I am astonished that you are so quickly deserting him who called you in the grace of Christ and are turning to a different gospel—not that there is another one, but there are some who trouble you and want to distort the gospel of Christ" (Gal 1:6–7). What is a false gospel?

A false gospel is news that parades itself as good while actually being sinister. A distorted, or false, gospel makes a deceitful promise and we sadly believe it. It's bad news disguised as good news that promises to give us what only the true gospel can. It entices us to put our hope and confidence in something other than Jesus and leads us to sin in all sorts of ways. No one sins out of duty. When tempted, we don't think: "I don't really want to sin, but I guess I have to lust, gossip, and boast." No, we sin because we perceive some benefit in the temptation. A false gospel sounds like these promises:

- "If you look lustfully, you'll experience relief and satisfaction."

- "If you spread gossip, you'll feel accepted by your friends."

- "If you keep your devotional time, God will be more pleased with you."

- "If you receive a lot of likes for that post, you'll be significant."

But false gospels never deliver on their promises. When we lust, we may experience a temporary rush or relief followed by an insatiable desire for more, a twinge of guilt, and an abiding emptiness. Moreover, acting on this sin leads to objectifying, dehumanizing, and oppressing others. Spreading gossip may make us feel accepted for a moment, while tearing apart our relationships. It nurtures proud distrust of others and unquestioning trust in ourselves. Silent boasting over "likes" might make us feel important for a few seconds, but it makes us dependent on approval from others, distancing us from lasting significance as a child of God.

False gospels make their appeals in various costumes. Some are cloaked in *performance*: Do this and you'll be accepted. Others look like *license*: Because God forgives, I'm free to do what I want. Another false gospel appeals to *independence*: Be true to yourself and you'll be happy. While there are many false gospels, let's take a closer look at these three.

RELIGIOUS PERFORMANCE

In the New Testament, the Galatians were deserting the true gospel in order to find acceptance from people they admired. Paul calls Peter out for his religious performance: "For before certain men came from James, he was eating with the Gentiles; but when they came he drew back and separated himself, fearing the circumcision party" (Gal 2:12). Observing the legalistic rules of Judaism, Peter separated himself from the Gentiles. Why? To be accepted by the religious.

Interestingly, people wooed by legalism don't think of themselves as performers; they think they're in the right. We seek affirmation, acceptance, and significance through rule-keeping, which breeds self-righteousness. Have you ever been in a conversation with a person who confessed their spiritual apathy or sin and thought, "I can't believe they're doing that!" This is a sign we're viewing others through our own religious performance instead of the gospel of grace.

Or perhaps you've felt insignificant because you haven't achieved more social justice, or you've failed to share the gospel, or you feel like you don't pray enough. Religious performance is a double-edged sword. It bloats us with pride when we succeed but mocks us with insults when we fail. Religious performance is a bad master.

Paul stands in contrast to Peter as someone who doesn't perform for approval. We seek people's approval often because of two powerful fears: we fear the isolation of rejection and we fear not being validated by the "in" group. So how does Paul resist these fears and this false gospel? By choosing to serve a better master: "If I were still trying to please man, I would not be a servant of Christ" (Gal 1:10). Because he is bound to Christ, Paul is freed from the approval of man to please Christ—he knows God's embrace and finds validation from God's call of grace. Indeed, Paul has found a more merciful and worthy master to serve. Consider the difference between performance as your master and master Jesus. What happens when we fail master Jesus? Does he mock us? No, he dies for us! Jesus calls us to turn around and face his grace.

In fact, it is Jesus's grace that leads Paul to perform, not *for* approval but *from* approval. Listen to what Paul says in 1 Corinthians 15:10, which we looked at in chapter 1: "I worked harder than any of them, though it was not I, but the grace of God that is with me." This illustrates what Dallas

Willard once wrote: "Grace is not opposed to effort, it is opposed to earning."[3]

Reflection: *Do you experience the bloating up of pride or the mocking of religious performance? Pause to confess your sin to Jesus and ask him to replace your motivations with his marvelous grace.*

SPIRITUAL LICENSE

It's commonly said that just as there were two thieves on the cross next to Jesus, there are two opposing threats to the gospel: there is the "ditch" of legalism, which relies on following the rules to earn God's favor. Then there is the "ditch" of licentious or license—historically called antinomianism—which relies on Jesus's salvific grace, making all our actions of little consequence.

Although it may come as a surprise, licentious people are also rule-centered. They prefer to break the rules, whereas performers keep the rules. One swerves right of the gospel; the other swerves left. Those who operate on spiritual license perceive themselves as liberated, set free from the

---

[3] J. P. Moreland and Dallas Willard, *Loving God with All Your Mind: The Role of Reason in the Life of the Soul* (Colorado Springs, CO: NavPress, 1997), 12.

bondage of more conservative Christians. But their view of freedom is distorted.

In Galatians 5, Paul lists some sins of spiritual license, including sexual immorality, strife, fits of anger, envy, and division (Gal 5:19–21). These works of the flesh are the result of going our own way. The sexually immoral reject God's design for sexual flourishing, damaging themselves and dishonoring others. The angry exalt their view over God's view, insisting on their preference over God's providence. The envious obsess over what others have instead of joyfully accepting what God has given.

This tendency to indulge the flesh is often justified by saying, "I don't want to be legalistic." But this exchanges one false gospel for another. The licentious define themselves as anti-legalist instead of *in Christ*. As a result, their identity is negatively formed instead of positively shaped through their union with Christ.

While religious performance and spiritual license are bad masters, Jesus is an infinitely good master who leads us into his rule and his way.

This was true for Brian. He lived under the banner of moral freedom, living a life of unrestrained drinking and lusting, which led to cheating on his wife and practicing an open marriage. But eventually this freedom caught up with him. His marriage ended in divorce, and his adult children refused to speak with him. After coming to Christ, he stood up at a men's retreat and shared his story, concluding with this comment, "If you think moral freedom is fun, come talk to me afterward. It will leave your life in shambles." Spiritual license will make a wreck of your life. First John 5:3 states that God's commandments are "not burdensome," for rather than leading us into self-destruction, they lead us into life.

License: "If I look lustfully, I will experience satisfaction and relief."
Gospel: "Blessed are the pure in heart, for they shall see God" (Matt 5:8).

License: "If I spread gossip, I will feel accepted by my friends."
Gospel: "Because God never gossips about me, I don't need to live for others' acceptance."

Performance: "If you keep your devotions, God will be more pleased with you."
Gospel: "Since God is already pleased with me in Christ, my devotional time is an invitation into more of his pleasure."

Performance: "If I receive a lot of likes for a post, I will be more significant."
Gospel: "Because I am eternally significant in Christ, I don't have to cherish likes."

INDEPENDENCE: EXPRESSIVE INDIVIDUALISM

A widely accepted false gospel that is a subset of spiritual license is *expressive individualism*. This view of the world believes "each person has a unique core of feeling and intuition that should unfold or be expressed if individuality is to be realized."[4] While expressive individualism partly avoids the trap of groupthink common in older generations, it goes too far by insisting an individual's core feeling should determine what is ethical.[5]

We encounter this false gospel in everyday life when we are counseled to "follow your heart," or "you do you." This advice can be helpful in understanding what we desire, but falsely assumes our desires are always right and good. Should we counsel emotionally abusive bosses to "you do you," or

[4] Robert N. Bellah, *Habits of the Heart: Individualism and Commitment in American Life* (Los Angeles: University of California Press, 1996), 333–34.

[5] Expressive individualism in a sense is another form of groupthink because no one can avoid being formed by others, and the widespread belief in expressive individuality has sadly become the norm for many of us.

militant dictators to "follow their heart"? Certainly not. It appears the heart is in need of an outside authority to guide us in making ethical and moral decisions.

Unfortunately, expressive individualism often eschews the laws of science, cultural tradition, government regulations, time-tested philosophies and religions, and churches. Ironically, that same suspicion is not turned onto the self. Instead, the individual is placed at the center of everything, free to form opinions without the help of tradition, divine revelation, or law.

Expressive Individualism and the Gospel

Part of the core problem of expressive individualism is what this belief centers on—us. Recall how we discussed in chapter 1 that the gospel is of first importance. Everything is meant to orbit around the gospel of Jesus like the planets orbit the sun. That is another way of saying the center of all things is meant to be God in his triune glory and grace. Expressive individualism centers on us instead of centering us in relation to God. The results are disastrous because we are not made to be the center of all things and we cannot withstand the pressure of all things relying on us.

Making ourselves the center through expressive individualism often harms communities and severs relationships. This upending of community is a threat both new and ancient. Notice how Paul exhorts Christians to live in community "with all humility and gentleness, with patience, bearing with one another in love, eager to maintain the unity of the Spirit in the bond of peace" (Eph 4:2–3). The center is not themselves but the attitudes and postures that flow from having the gospel at the center of their lives.

How, then, does the true gospel address this false gospel of expressive individualism? Expressive individualism says, "Take up your cause and follow self." Jesus says, "I have taken up the cross for you. Now take up your cross and follow me." In expressive individualism we are *slaves to self.* Because of the gospel, our identity is now *servants of Christ.* Therefore, Christians should recognize Jesus and his word as the chief authority of their lives, not their personal feelings, passions, or preferences. When we strive together to honor Jesus as Lord, the church's primary witness will be the glory of Christ not the glory of our individual preferences or passions.

While there are many false gospels, each one gives us an opportunity to cherish the true gospel by realizing its innate goodness. By examining the deceitful claims of other beliefs, we can demonstrate the veracity and beauty of "the faith that was once for all delivered to the saints" (Jude 3). May God help us defend ourselves and others from Satan's schemes with a deeper grasp of the gospel.

FOR FURTHER REFLECTION

Read and reflect *on the following passages, considering both the original author's intent and meaning, as well as the text's connection to the chapter's topic.*

Galatians 1:6-7   Galatians 5:16-24   Matthew 16:24-25

Discussion questions

1. How can 'false gospels' harm us?

2. This chapter focused on 3 false gospels - religious performance, spiritual license, and independence. Which one have or do you personally struggle with the most? What does that look like?

3. How does the gospel keep us from both legalism and license? How does the gospel change why we obey, or why we don't disobey?

4. How is the gospel better news than expressive individualism?

CHAPTER 6

IN STEP WITH
THE GOSPEL

We have considered the preeminence of the gospel, its doctrinal richness, and appropriate responses to the good news. We've already seen a number of ways the glorious gospel of God's grace can become distorted. How false gospels can creep in, hold us hostage, and do their worst. But false gospels are not the only enemy. In this chapter, we will explore how gospel faith is meant to produce communities marked by gospel culture. The gospel changes how we see the world (belief) *and* how we relate to others (culture).

One of the best ways to learn how gospel doctrine leads to gospel culture is to see how easily this *doesn't* happen. In Galatians 2, we read of a conflict between two apostolic church leaders, Peter and Paul. The conflict wasn't over competing doctrines (orthodoxy) but corrupt behavior (orthopraxy). Peter, one of the pillars of the church, was called out by Paul because his "conduct was not in step with the truth of the gospel." His behavior contradicted the gospel, as we'll unpack briefly in the sections below. He had the right belief but the wrong behavior.

The same danger exists for us. Will our churches, homes, and relationships declare the gospel in words but deny the gospel in behavior? Admittedly, this concept of getting the doctrine of the gospel right but getting the culture of the gospel wrong can feel abstract. To help illustrate, listen to how Francis Schaeffer captured this idea:

> One cannot explain the explosive power of the early church apart from the fact that they practiced two things simultaneously: the orthodoxy of doctrine and orthodoxy of community in the midst of the visible church, a community which the world could see. By the grace of God, therefore, the church must be known simultaneously for its purity of doctrine and the reality of its community. Our churches have so often been only preaching points with very little emphasis on community. But the exhibition of the love of God in practice is beautiful and must be there.[6]

---

[6] Francis Schaeffer, *The Church At the End of the 20th Century* (Wheaton, IL: Crossway, 1971), 144.

The section title in which Schaeffer's writes this is instructive: *The Church Before the Watching World.* It is our sacred privilege to display orthodoxy of belief and orthopraxy of community before each other and the world. Jesus said the world will know us by our love (John 13:35); we must walk in step with the gospel that changes our beliefs and our culture.

WALKING IN LINE
WITH THE GOSPEL

Let's return to Galatians 2 and examine what this passage teaches us about gospel doctrine and culture. As we stated earlier, the confrontation between Peter and Paul was not over doctrines but behavior. Paul calls Peter out because his "conduct was not in step with the truth of the gospel" (Gal 2:14). The phrase "not in step" comes from the Greek word *orthopodeo*, from which we get "orthopedic." It emphasizes straight or correct conduct that aligns with the gospel. What was Peter doing that was out of step with the gospel? Here's what Paul records in Galatians 2:12–13:

> For before certain men came from James, he was eating with the Gentiles; but when they came he drew back and separated himself, fearing the circumcision party. And

> the rest of the Jews acted hypocritically along with him,
> so that even Barnabas was led astray by their hypocrisy.

Peter exemplified crooked conduct by withdrawing from eating with Gentile Christians and prioritizing fellowship with Jewish Christians. Before influential Jewish Christians like James came to town, Peter had no problem eating with Gentile Christians. But that all changed when Jewish Christians (the circumcision group) arrived. Modern Western readers may think this is just a first-century version of high school lunch-time drama. How exactly is Peter's behavior out of line with the truth of the gospel?

Here's what was at stake: Peter denied by his actions the very gospel he proclaimed with his words. When Peter withdrew from eating with Gentile believers, he reinforced the idea that the keeping of kosher dietary laws was necessary to be fully accepted by God. In addition to propagating "justification by works" through his behavior, Peter reinforced ethnic and ritual boundary markers that effectively created an A and B team within the church. So Paul rebukes Peter by saying he stood condemned (2:11).

Why did Paul use such strong language? Because Peter's actions were out of line with the truth of the gospel. They were a clear denial of the gospel that we are saved by grace through faith in Jesus alone, not by works or what we do. Peter's actions subverted the primary aim of the gospel to justify people before God in Christ. Peter's misstep wasn't primarily cultural (Christians must keep Jewish custom); it was doctrinal (Christians have to keep Jewish custom to be justified). Therefore, Paul says, "I saw that their conduct was not in step with the truth of the gospel" (2:14), not "I saw their conduct was not in step with cultural norms." Peter's table actions denied the very gospel he preached.

"It is possible for us today to unsay by our church culture what we say by our church doctrine. Which means we can defeat the advance of the gospel, however biblical our exposition and however brilliant our apologetics, by the conduct we display and the social dynamics we create with one another."[7]

THE POWER OF GOSPEL COMMUNITY

Note that Peter's misstep led others to behave as he did: "And the rest of the Jews acted hypocritically along with him,

---

[7] Ray Ortlund, "GOSPEL DOCTRINE, GOSPEL CULTURE, GOSPEL SPIRITUALITY" https://summitcollaborative.org/gospel-doctrine-gospel-culture-gospel-spirituality/

so that even Barnabas was led astray by their hypocrisy" (Gal 2:13). But the opposite can be true as well—walking in step with the gospel can lead others to see and experience Christ in doctrine and in culture.

When we truly internalize the gospel of grace, it transforms the culture of our churches, our relationships, and our witness to the world. Consider how Ray Ortlund captures this idea:

> Gospel doctrine creates a gospel culture. The doctrine of grace creates a culture of grace. When the doctrine is clear and the culture is beautiful, that church will be powerful. But there are no shortcuts to getting there. Without the doctrine, the culture will be weak. Without the culture, the doctrine will seem pointless.[8]

Orthodoxy of doctrine and orthodoxy of culture are necessary if we are to honor the gospel. We need both. Healthy doctrine produces a distinct community culture, and distinct community reinforces and displays right doctrine. Doctrine sustains a vibrant, Christ-centered community because it shows us the glory of Jesus and teaches us how to reflect him. A distinct community calls attention to this Jesus, and when asked for the reason behind the way they live, it points back

---

[8] Ray Ortlund, *The Gospel: How the Church Portrays the Beauty of Christ* (Wheaton, IL, Crossway, 2014), 21.

to Jesus. When these two orthodoxies are in sync, it produces a beautiful and believable expression of the gospel.

BEAUTIFUL AND BELIEVABLE GOSPEL EXPRESSIONS

When our doctrine and our culture are in sync through the gospel, beautiful and believable expressions of Christ's power and grace come alive in our relationships. Consider these two examples of what it looks like when gospel doctrine and gospel culture are aligned.

First, a personal example. When I met my neighbor Geoff at a birthday party, he described himself as "spiritual but not religious." We connected over movies, and I left praying for him. The next time I saw Geoff, we picked up where we left off. He asked me who all the people were at the prior party, and I explained that a lot of them were part of my church. Intrigued by their character, he asked more about the church.

As I explained the difference between the gospel and religion, Geoff resonated, so I invited him to join our small group for dinner. Over the meal, he connected with Luke, who had a master's degree in sociology. The two of them hit it off analyzing cultural trends, and they began hanging out. Luke helped Geoff see that you don't have to be anti-intellectual to be a Christian. In fact, Christianity has a rich history of faith seeking understanding. Eventually, Geoff joined us on a Sunday, and within months of hearing the gospel, he put his faith in Jesus.

What drew Geoff to Christ? It wasn't a lone evangelistic voice but a chorus of voices reflecting the beauty and grace of Jesus. Whether it was at the social function, or in a small group, Geoff encountered the power of a community shaped by the gospel.

A second example of gospel doctrine and culture comes from a story Jesus told. In Luke 15:11–32, Jesus tells the story of the prodigal son. In the parable, the younger son demands his inheritance from his father while his father is still living, a request that shows his absolute disregard for his father. It's hard to think of a more grievous act in a patriarchal society. The father obliges, and the younger son goes to the city and squanders everything in a flurry of hedonism. The younger son hits rock bottom and decides to go home to his father. Knowing how deeply he has betrayed his father and family, the younger son plans to go home as a slave since he knows he can never be accepted again as a son. As he approaches home, the younger son is shocked by what he sees:

> But while he was still a long way off, his father saw him and felt compassion, and ran and embraced him and kissed him. And the son said to him, "Father, I have sinned

against heaven and before you. I am no longer worthy to be called your son." But the father said to his servants, "Bring quickly the best robe, and put it on him, and put a ring on his hand, and shoes on his feet. And bring the fattened calf and kill it, and let us eat and celebrate. For this my son was dead, and is alive again; he was lost, and is found." (Luke 15:20b–24)

This parable is enacted grace. The father's embrace of the son preaches with the force of one thousand sermons on forgiveness—all in one act. The parable shows the power of gospel culture, a culture that we can embody in our churches, homes, and relationships. Because the Father has embraced us in radical grace, we too can share that grace with others by how we treat one another.

A healthy church is unlike every other collectivity on earth. A healthy church lives in the all-sufficient grace of God in Christ, equally shared, by all alike, through faith alone, so that diverse people can be who they are in Christ.

SHAPING COMMUNITIES
WITH THE GOSPEL

How do Christian communities become formed by the gospel in doctrine and in culture? Just as we looked at two examples of beautiful and believable gospel culture at work in the section above, we'll look at two ways gospel culture can be formed. Above we looked at the what and now we turn to the how.

Knowledge and Experience of the Gospel

The primary way communities can grow in gospel culture is to know and display the grace we have received. In other words, a gospel culture must have for its foundation people who know the gospel—that while we were still sinners Christ died for the ungodly (Rom 5:8). Knowing this deep in our bones helps us to forgive as we are forgiven (Eph 4:32b) and to welcome others as Christ welcomed us (Rom 15:7).

The transformative effects of knowing and experiencing the gospel are powerfully displayed in Jesus's parable in Luke 15:11–32, which we discussed earlier. However, the parable includes one character we did not mention: the elder brother. When the younger brother is embraced by the father, the elder brother is deeply angered because he feels all his obedience has been overlooked. The father responds graciously to the elder brother's self-righteousness, which leads many to speak of this parable as the parable of the prodigal sons. The parable is about two *sons* lost by two different false gospels.

In chapter 5, we identified legalism and license as two enemies of the gospel. We can see this duality in the parable of the prodigal sons—the older brother is *legalistic* (believing in a works-righteousness) and the younger brother is *licentious* (believing flourishing is found by following self). As those who are likely a mix of both elder- and younger-brother brokenness, our journey is to move away from legalism and license and, through the embrace of the father, to become like *the* Father. This means our experience and knowledge of God's grace should lead us to live as people who bring the embrace of the gospel to others.

Here are two examples of how this could be shown in real life. A mom can be an embodiment of Christ to her young children. To respond with grace and patience to a wayward child is to bring gospel culture to life. A friend who hears a peer confess sin and responds without shock and disgust but with a word of gospel comfort and wisdom has created gospel culture. Of course, no one will do this perfectly. But even in our failure to be like the Father, we continually receive grace while learning more and more of what it means to embody the grace of Christ. The Father's grace transforms us to be more like him.

Intentional Community Practices

A second way gospel cultures can be formed is through intentional communal practices—practices that help us know
and apply the gospel together. Some churches use "house
rules" to train their communities by codifying what grace
looks like in pithy statements. Others use gospel rhythms,
and some emphasize missional practices. What all of these
have in common is intentionality. They structure and train
their churches to become vibrant communities of gospel
practice and culture.

In Acts, the apostles intentionally emphasized three key
things: apostolic teaching, fellowship, and gospel witness.

> And they devoted themselves to the apostles' teaching
> and the fellowship, to the breaking of bread and the
> prayers. And awe came upon every soul, and many won-
> ders and signs were being done through the apostles.
> And all who believed were together and had all things
> in common. And they were selling their possessions and
> belongings and distributing the proceeds to all, as any
> had need. And day by day, attending the temple together
> and breaking bread in their homes, they received their
> food with glad and generous hearts, praising God and
> having favor with all the people. And the Lord added to
> their number day by day those who were being saved.
> (Acts 2:42–47)

The *apostolic teaching* was an outworking of what the apostles learned from Jesus—a Christ-centered understanding of the Scriptures (Luke 24:44–48). This rich, doctrinal emphasis was united with *fellowship*: sharing meals, prayers, and possessions. Their life together spilled over in *mission*: concern for the poor, gathered worship, and evangelistic witness. These early communities were so distinct that people joined their number daily. These Christians were shaped by a commitment to the gospel, community, and mission. As a result, they had both good gospel doctrine and good gospel culture.

The radical nature of the Acts community may be intimidating. Share my possessions? Eat meals with others regularly? Invite strangers into my home? Modern individuals are often out of step with the biblical vision of community. Our lives can be so career driven or family focused that we miss out on being the distinct, provocative people of God.

COMMUNITY PRACTICES

Now that we have considered the power of living in gospel community, let's consider some practices that can help foster a gospel culture in these communities. While you do not have to copy and paste them into your own setting, you do need to be intentional about what you are doing to live out the gospel with others.

At the beginning of every year, our missional community takes time to reflect on the three core values of Acts 2:42–47. We ask ourselves: What would it look like for us to grow as a gospel people this year? How can we mature as a family? How are we doing as a missionary community? Here are some examples of commitments made by our communities:

GOSPEL PEOPLE

- Let's all make sure we are in vibrant discipleship relationships this year and commit to regularly reading the Bible with a couple of friends.

- When people confess their sins in our group, let's ask God to give us compassion and wisdom in our responses.

- We've allowed our shared meal time to crowd out sermon discussion, so let's keep an eye on the clock so we can all encounter Christ in his Word.

COMMUNITY PEOPLE

- We've had trouble connecting beyond our weekly meeting time, so let's commit to one social event each month. It will be fun!

- With two babies coming this year, let's be sure to put a meal calendar together for those families.

- Some of us have been hit hard by the recession, so let's create an emergency fund to pool some resources to help one another out.

- Although we pray at the end of every meeting, we could spend more time taking our needs and longings to God. Why don't we dedicate an evening to prayer each quarter this year?

MISSIONARY PEOPLE

- Let's discuss the objections to Christianity our coworkers bring up and spend time praying for them.

- When we have our monthly social event, let's invite neighbors and friends.

- We're doing a great job serving meals each month at the local shelter, but let's try to initiate more conversations and pray for residents on the spot.

In order to intentionally cultivate these commitments over the course of a year, the community pulls them out every quarter to reflect on their progress. It's important to celebrate where we have followed through and give glory to God. Where we've struggled, we can encourage one another or even repent of selfish indifference.

TENSION
IN COMMUNITY

However, if we read Acts 2 in isolation from the rest of the book, we will idealize its description. Pastor and martyr Dietrich Bonhoeffer describes the "wish dream" that everyone brings into a community: "He who loves his dream of a community more than the Christian community itself becomes a destroyer of the latter."[9] What is your wish dream of community?

We may fixate on our group's performance in gospel, community, or mission. Blessings can quickly turn into burdensome expectations. For this reason, it is important to keep reading in Acts, where we observe the same community sinning and struggling. Reading Acts 2 in tandem with Acts 5, we witness the challenges of greed, lying, and death in cultivating gospel community.

The truth is all communities are comprised of people with deep, unmet longings and sinful demands. When our wishes aren't met, it may be tempting to slander our group or even leave. But these struggles are actually when real community can begin.

---

[9] Dietrich Bonhoeffer, *Life Together: The Classic Exploration of Faith in Community* (New York: HarperCollins, 1954), 27.

Jane was a passionate, articulate, and outspoken member of our group. She served faithfully in our mercy ministry and was quick to sympathize with those who struggled. However, whenever she didn't like something, she was quick to voice her complaint. One evening, she clashed with another member of the group during our sermon discussion. A few weeks later she called me to announce that she and her husband were leaving the group to find a community they connected with more naturally.

I expressed sympathy for her struggles and then asked her if the conflict had anything to do with her decision. After some honest conversation about her concerns, and Christ's call to leave our gift at the altar and reconcile with a brother (Matt 18:15), I graciously challenged her decision to leave. I reminded her that we were a spiritual family, and that healthy families talk through conflict. She conceded and agreed to pursue reconciliation.

Bonhoeffer exhorts Christians to become disillusioned with their *ideal of community* before they can enter into *the real community*. Only then can true community begin to take root. As it turned out, Jane was projecting the high expectations she had for herself onto others. But after receiving grace in her own failures, she learned to relax her expectations of others.

We are not alone in our struggle to live out this vision of community, but each struggle is an opportunity to return to Jesus for forgiveness, reconciliation, and transformation. In fact, it is important to remind one another that *tension in relationships is God's appointed grace for our change*. Very often, this is how God beautifies his people. So let's open ourselves up to the community he has given us, warts and all, in order to be transformed by his free-flowing grace. Then we will attract a watching world to Jesus, both in our doctrine and culture.

FOR FURTHER REFLECTION

Read and reflect *on the following passages, considering both the original author's intent and meaning, as well as the text's connection to the chapter's topic.*

John 13:35   Galatians 2:11-14   Luke 15:11-32

Discussion questions

1. Can you think of a time when the Gospel became more real to you because of how someone responded to your sin or treated you? What happened? Do did it reinforce the Gospel with you?

2. Why is Gospel culture important? How can it reflect, or undermine, gospel doctrine?

3. Read Romans 8:1. What would a church that believes Romans 8:1 feel like?

4. What intentional practice(s) could help you or your church reflect the gospel?

NOW I WOULD REMIND YOU

Although we have covered a lot of ground regarding the gospel and how it truly changes everything, there are many more depths to explore. As a final word, reflect again on the victory God has won for us through the saving work of Jesus:

> Jesus defeated the penalty of our sin, the power of death, and the presence of evil. Sin is forgiven through Jesus's substitutionary death in our place. Death is subverted by his resurrection life, which will eventually manifest into

a whole harvest of resurrections. Evil is cut off at the source, and put on notice, until Jesus returns to destroy every sinister authority. This is news the world so desperately wants: victory over sin, death, and evil!

All hearts yearn for this triumph. Consider, for example, the growing awareness of systemic corruption and evil in our society: political scandals, financial corruption, social isolation, racial prejudice, and political polarization—we are facing the cold truth that things are not what they ought to be.

Moreover, our awareness of this pervasive brokenness is matched by another harsh reality: even through our best activism and efforts, we are unable to bring deep, lasting change. We sense the need for deliverance and victory but are unable to be our own victors.

However, the victory of Christ is real and resplendent. His triumph is future and present. It is changing individuals, families, communities, cities, countries, and the entire world. Take heart, the gospel is the good and true story that Jesus has defeated sin, death, and evil through his own death and resurrection. He is making all things new, even us!

We began this book in the first few verses of 1 Corinthians 15. It seems only right to finish it with the final verses of that incredible chapter.

I tell you this, brothers: flesh and blood cannot inherit the kingdom of God, nor does the perishable inherit the imperishable. Behold! I tell you a mystery. We shall not all sleep, but we shall all be changed, in a moment, in the twinkling of an eye, at the last trumpet. For the trumpet will sound, and the dead will be raised imperishable, and we shall be changed. For this perishable body must put on the imperishable, and this mortal body must put on immortality. When the perishable puts on the imperishable, and the mortal puts on immortality, then shall come to pass the saying that is written:

"Death is swallowed up in victory."
"O death, where is your victory?
O death, where is your sting?"

The sting of death is sin, and the power of sin is the law. But thanks be to God, who gives us the victory through our Lord Jesus Christ.

Therefore, my beloved brothers, be steadfast, immovable, always abounding in the work of the Lord, knowing that in the Lord your labor is not in vain. (15:50-58)

KEY
PROJECT

Each Foundations book includes a key project, or two, to help you synthesize what you have learned. We encourage you to complete it now if you haven't already, and then discuss it at your final group gathering. There is one project for this book.

Written Personal Definition of the Gospel and Personal Testimony in Light of It

Write a definition of the gospel that is in your own words, but that also takes your learnings from the book into account. Additionally, write your personal testimony in such a way that it becomes a real-life demonstration of your personal definition of the gospel.

Made in the USA
Coppell, TX
29 November 2024

41277206R00062